Dedication

This book is dedicated to Donny. He was a friend and a brother since our early childhood, and passed away in 2010. Donny believed in me, and he wanted me to continue with my work to show others that we do live on after death. After his burial, he communicated to me to go back to the cemetery the next evening and take a few pictures. Donny wanted me to show his parents and family this picture to assure them that he was fine. Below is Donny as promised, in his favorite Pittsburgh Steelers shirt.

COPYRIGHT

Copyright © by Ghost Visions, LLC

All photographs © photo by Ghost Visions, LLC

All rights reserved. No part of this book may be reproduced by any mechanical, photographic, or electronic process, or in the form of a phonographic recording; nor may it be stored in a retrieval system, transmitted, or otherwise be copied for public or private use. No part of this book may be used without prior written permission of the publisher or author. The intent of the author is only to offer information of a general nature to help you in your quest for spiritual well-being. In the event you use any of the information in this book for yourself, which is your constitutional right, the author and the publisher assume no responsibility for your actions

Library of Congress Cataloging- in Publication Data

**ISBN-13:
978-1537067179**

**ISBN-10:
1537067176**

CONTENTS

Dedication..
About Spirit Photography 4
Why are spirits still here 5
Why are some pictures blurry 6
Woodsboro - Rocky Hill Cemetery...................................8
The National Museum of Civil War Medicine..............11
Utica Covered Bridge 15
Haunted Historical New Market....................................17
Gabriel's Inn Restaurant..22
Fort Frederick State Park..33
Landon House...35
Mount Saint Mary's..39
Catoctin Furnace...42
Monocacy National Battlefield.......................................49

ABOUT SPIRIT PHOTOGRAPHY

My Goal is to bring Spirit Photography back into focus to show that there is life after death and that your soul does live on.

Back in the late 1800's to early 1900's Spirit Photography got a lot of bad publicity for those who tried to trick the public with their enhanced photographs, this lead to of years of negativity and disbelief in anyone who captured a ghost/spirit in a photograph or video in the name of "Spirit Photography".

Spirits want you to know they exist and there is life after death. You don't have to be a psychic or highly evolved being to be curious about the afterlife and to capture the spirits in photographs that are trying to communicate to all of us.

By bringing Spirit Photography back into focus, I have taught others who have been very successful at capturing spirits in their photos, armed only with their personal cameras.

Teaching this lost art of communicating with the spirits that still reside with us has given hope, belief and peace that once our bodies fail us we do still exist.

In the next few pages are photographs of actual spirits in full form taken by Ghost Visions, LLC.

Why are spirits still here?

Spirits are stuck in the middle "by choice" in what is known as being "Earthbound". You are not told what to do; it is always what path you want to lead at your choosing.

Some of those reasons for remaining Earthbound are:

1. Feeling unworthy to move into the light or

2. They come from a background where they were taught that anything they did bad (swearing, drinking etc) was spiritually wrong and they would go to hell if they were not pure of spirit.

3. Some are afraid of the light and they don't know what it is. If they do go they wonder if they will be punished.

4. Other spirits do not realize that they are dead. These are deaths that were very quick and unexpected.

5. Angels and guides will stay Earthbound for periods of time trying to help others to pass over to the light and not to be afraid.

6. The spirits of loved ones are waiting to pass over with their family or friend.

7. A lot of souls have some message or unfinished business to resolve before they feel that they can cross over to the light.

Lastly, two spirits who were soul mates, explained that they would rather spend the rest of their existence together earthbound, then to cross over into the unknown and have to be separated by any means.

Why are some pictures blurry?

The spirit realms are invisible to some of us and exist in another "place". The phrase I use for this is the "Veil Between Worlds".

When taking spirit photographs, it's like an art form and you're actually stepping, for a brief moment in time, into their reality. That's when you capture the photograph. Spirits start out as a ball of energy and then can manifest to full form. You don't need a special camera or ghost hunting equipment. I always get a surprise look when I'm asked what camera I use to get such precise pictures. I only use my Kodak digital camera (Easy Share), but any camera can produce the same results. It's not the kind of equipment you need; it's the person behind the equipment knowing how to use his or her own energy in capturing spirits/ghosts in your photographs. But that subject of for another time. Some other factors I have learned in recent years are as follows:

1. On our tours we have captured orbs in motion, sometimes they are precise and others are blurry. This is because spirits are always on the move and active.

2. It depends on temperature and time of day that pictures are taken. On cool days the pictures are clearer than on hot days.

3. The results between a focused and blurry picture depends on the energy level of the person taking the picture. When spirits go from orb to full form, they will use your energy and sometimes drain the energy from your batteries of your camera or cell phone. This is why sometimes your camera will shut down when taking a picture, but once you leave the area it will work again. If you are tired and low on energy you will not get a clear picture.

4. The veil that is between our world and theirs is very heavy at times and has its own fluctuations, like our weather conditions.

5. You will notice in some pictures the spirit or figures are clear and the rest of the picture is blurry, or the surroundings are clear and the spirit is blurry. This is all due to the timing of getting the picture through the veil of time when all of the surroundings are just coming into focus.

In this picture, the front is blurry, but you can see a tree in the background that is clear and in focus. This is an example of looking through into other realm.

TURN THE PAGE TO START YOU JOURNEY!

Legend of Woodsboro - Rocky Hill Cemetery

There is a tombstone in Rocky Hill Cemetery that bleeds. The woman it belongs to told her husband if he remarries and his new wife is cruel to her children her tombstone will bleed. They have changed the tombstone several times and the blood keeps coming back. **They have an inscription in front of her tombstone that reads:** *"This stone is at the grave of a mother who died leaving several small children. The husband remarried as husbands do, and tis' said that he and the stepmother were very cruel and unkind to the children, but Death could not this mother's anguish kill, when the knarled oaks groan, and the pine trees moan, in this grave yard at Rocky Hill, the tale often told on many a lonely stretch, is that this stone breaks out in bloody sweats, in this grave yard at Rocky Hill".*
The cemetery is located in Woodsboro on Coppermine Road. The tombstone is located in the left hand corner third row back in the middle of the row bearing the names of George and Mary Fox. Local Legend posted from the shadowlands.net

We picked this local legend to investigate because we felt that this would be an active location during the full moon that night. I can report that this site had some very unusual disturbances, the energy felt negative and unstable, the kind you would want to run from.

It is unusual that I could not get a clear picture in any of my photos, but you could tell our visit was not welcomed that night. Cindy, who is a long time Ghost Visions, LLC member, felt the same disturbance as I did and she could not get a clear picture either.

We did find the stone of Mary Fox, it did not bleed that night (full moon), but you can see stains that looked pinkish in color. What we did find in our photographs were several souls at an eerie site.

I have to say that I not sure of the grave stone in the legend below, but this graveyard in general pass as Ghost Visions, LLC Legend of paranormal activity. The energy there was very threatening; you won't see me there any time soon.

Circled is a face of a man over his head stone above.

Below right behind the orb in the middle you can see several spirits; one man (by the tree) is wearing his tie and suit that he was buried in. You can see the other spirits coming into focus on the left side of the picture wearing what looks like robes. They were all walking away from us towards the light. Don't miss the other spirits located on the upper right edge of this picture.

Legend of The National Museum of Civil War Medicine

The museum is known to be the home of seven ghosts or more. One ghost was the undertaker's assistant who once worked in the building. There is another ghost who was a railroad worker who job was to transport the soldier bodies to the mortuary. A number of civil war soldiers are also known to haunt this building. Some of the ghost haunting the museum seems to be haunting objects in the museum that belong to them when they were alive. Local Legend posted from the Frederickghost.blogspot.com

The National Museum of Civil War Medicine was our first haunted investigation site. Ghost Visions was given special permission to investigate behind the scenes to prove that the legend of ghosts/spirits were indeed haunting the museum. There was a strong presence of spirit energy as we were taken on our tour throughout the building.

We found that the upper floor camp area had the most spirit activity.
Our investigation group was all together in another room with the guide when I felt the spirits presence coming into the camp area room. I ran from the location we currently were investigating to the camp area which resulted in the picture on the next page.

This site has a lot of spirits who were attached to the civil war items on display. The earthbound soldiers are attracted to the home like environment that they once knew.

Next to the manikin circled on the right side, is a spirit that materialized and came into focus, you can see his beard and part of his hat and uniform as he looks at the spirit in the middle. Actually, at first I did not see the spirit in the middle of the picture until The National Civil War Museum sent me an email saying they found another spirit I over looked.

Their comments were best said in the following: Very interesting pictures. Thanks for sending them my way. I think that the most interesting picture is # 5. If you look very carefully below one of the images you circled, you can see what appears to be a confederate soldier in grey clad uniform. He is sitting between the two soldiers in the middle, sitting around the fire.

It looks like he has an officer's stripe on his trousers and a glint off of the spot where his gold shirt buttons would have been. The image also appears to have his legs crossed. The image you circled above this appears to be a bearded face that is partially blocked by one of the manikins.

In Spirit Photography you always double click when taking the picture so you can get the spirits progress in coming into full focus. Below is the second picture I took in this direction where the bearded solider that materialized on the right side of the manikin came into full figure.

Legend of Utica Covered Bridge, Utica, Maryland

Local Legend: A young boy drowned in the deep water a long time ago. People reported that his ghost haunts the bridge. One evening a couple was returning home from Frederick when their car approached the bridge, they noticed a thick fog rising from the river. The driver turned on his headlights to dim so that he could see better. About halfway over the bridge, the car's headlights caught the figure of a young boy and his hair and clothes were dripping wet. The driver slammed on his brakes and the car slid to a stop on the wet planking after apparently striking the boy. The driver jumped from his vehicle and fell to his knees and looked under the car, no one was there. The driver got the eerie feeling that he was being watched and he turned to look toward the rear of the car. The boy that he had just hit was standing there, watching him with blank and staring eyes. The man started to speak, and the boy slowly faded away into the darkness.

The first time I was at this site was with a ghost tour group. I wondered off in my own direction where I felt spirit energy and had gotten my first recording (EVP) of a boy saying "Don't go on the bridge, please don't", which is on my Ghost Visions Facebook page. When I went back to the site a week later to investigate further, I felt that the spirits were really reluctant to come out and communicate. I got back into my car and was at the top of the hill, when I felt that the spirits were materializing. I got out of my car and took the picture below. When I zoomed in on the picture, I saw that I had captured two spirits of the children on the bridge.

Circled below is the spirits of a boy and girl. The boy is leaning against the tree in a red shirt and he is looking down at the girl below him who is squatting down and looking towards the bridge.

Legends of Haunted Historical New Market

There's not a single thing extraordinary concerning New Market, Maryland while the sun shines, but this town is run by the living dead after the sun has called it a day. Spirits are so regular in this town that local residents don't even think about it anymore, the undead spirits of New Market are all too real. Ghost Visions have had several ghost tours throughout the years and each one is different, you never know what spirits you capture in your photographs along the way. .

Go to: www.ghostofamerica.com for some of the ghost stories in the area. **More photographs and haunted stories are in our book dedicated to New Market called "Haunted Historical New Market, Maryland".**

Below I captured a solider (captain) walking towards the entrance of the house and on top of the roof kneeling was another spirit dressed in white. This was at the Strawberry Inn on Main Street.

In this picture is a face of a man looking at me from around the tree, a boy sitting in the tree by the flag and a little girl down from him peaking at me from the base of the tree.

This picture was taken Christmas Eve 2006 in the town of New Market. Below and circled is a little girl sitting on the chair and smiling.

An angel was captured in the window at Ben's "Santa Fe Trading" in New Market.

Legends of Gabriel's Inn Restaurant

Summer ghost tour offers tales and scares

(Article from the Gazette News Post)

Sean Delawder and his wife, Shirl, own Gabriel's Inn restaurant. But soon they found something interesting. "We found out about the ghosts through our own experiences," Sean Delawder said. "And by speaking with customers and our tenants who have had experiences." These experiences gave birth to the idea of sharing their ghostly "residents" with the public.

Manseau is a spirit photographer with Ghost Visions, LLC of New Market. She can sense where spirits assemble, and take pictures to see if anything of interest shows itself. Manseau herself said she had the sense since she was a child and that she can also pick up names when she is searching. The Delawders allowed them to take photos and film videos. Manseau expected to find orbs, little balls of light that many claim to be spirits, in their photos. What they found they wanted to share with everyone. These photos gave birth to the first ever summer ghost tours. During the Civil War, the building was used as a hospital for the North and the South. In 1896, it was turned into a sanitarium for women with mild mental disorders. According to Shirl Delawder, in 1968, Guy Gabriel bought the property and turned it into Gabriel's French Provincial Inn and raised a family.

In 1998, the DeLawder family purchased the property from the Gabriel estate. Before the show began, Manseau told the audience that the more open-minded they were, the more they would see. "Some of you will even see more than me," she said. The slideshow itself consisted of many photos outside of Gabriel's Inn

Sometimes portions of the photos were highlighted to show the figure more fully, and other times it showed close ups of the areas in question. As they went through the photos, they explained about the different ghosts living on the grounds. They said one is a child named Joshua who is the mischievous spirit of the group who enjoys playing harmless jokes and pranks. Many of the images were small, even if they show full-figured beings. One photo clearly showed a face, while others showed figures and faces hiding themselves in the surrounding forest, or even beams of light. When the slideshow ended, the walking tour began. Sometimes at dawn, Delawder said she heard horses neighing and dogs barking and men yelling around the area. "It sounds like a battle," she said. But whenever she looked, there was nothing. Gathered in the dining room, the group commented on their experiences.

As first-timer Tracy Beeman walked the tour, she said she felt someone, like a child, holding her hand all the way through it. "Sometimes people can see more in the photos than others," Manseau said. "The more open you are, the more they will interact with you and show themselves."

Copyright©2010 Post-Newsweek Media, Inc./Gazette.Net Thursday July 27, 2006 by Joshua Boehman Special to The Gazette

Since that time, new private owners have taken over what was Gabriel's Inn. You can drive passed the property, but please respect their privacy. This legend is true since I started my first ghost tours at this inn. The article is from the local gazette new paper that had participated in the tour that night. The inn has several spirits that inhabit inside and outside of the inn. Sometime we would hear horses, children screaming, drumming of marching soldiers and so much more. So yes, this inn is haunted with such a diverse history.

I have a lot of pictures from this Inn, but these are the best of them. As I was eating dinner in the smaller dining room with some friends, I was compelled to go into the large dining room (which was empty at the time) and take the below picture of the spirit troops who were marching up to the Inn. Below in the first window to the left, are the soldiers marching in a line towards the Inn. In the window to the right was an African American boy looking inside dressed in his death shroud.

This is a shed on the back of the property that is very haunted. As you can see below there were several ghosts that appeared when I took this picture. There is always some kind of spirit activity around this area. At our last summer ghost tour, several people on the tour heard a little girl scream which came from the direction of the shed. The spirit of the little girl has been spotted by this shed several times by others on our tours. Here you'll find to the left in the" V "branch of the tree is just the face of a little girl who seems to be yelling. Below the girl to her right is an Indian Spirit and floating out of the window is a spirit of a women. At the front door of the shed is a monk walking inside of the shed. As you look towards the peak of the shed, you can see a spirit flying by. Outside to the right of the shed is a young solider holding a rifle.

I usually do not get clear pictures at night, but as you can see below there were a lot of spirits in this picture. Up front is a boy named Joshua with blonde hair wearing a vest and jacket. Several spirits of women materialized on the porch and to the right of the bushes was a couple scolding two little girls with their backs to us. When the Owners of Gabriel's Inn took me for a tour, we stopped by the front of the Inn to find that all her gazing balls were tipped over. When the owner tried to put her glass down on the bench to pick them up, there was a force that kept pushing her back and would not let her set her drink down. When we continued the tour, I could feel Joshua behind me waving his arms out saying "I got you!", I then turned quickly and took this photo and said "Now, I got you!"

This pictures is what you would see when people talk about helping the spirits cross over. There are so many spirits in this picture. At the top right, appeared heavenly spirits helping the lost souls pass into the light. I named this picture "Heaven's Gate". Below is the original photograph and in the next couple of pictures is a breakdown of certain parts, so you can view the spirits clearly.

On the back patio at the table with his back to us, is a mischievous spirit of the Inn called "Joshua" blonde hair, white collar and blue velvet suit. Across from Joshua is another spirit of a boy talking to him. To the right of them is the spirit of a large dog and underneath the table to the left is a little girl with long braids. To the right of the girl with braids is a puppy. Below are two different views, the bottom is enhanced and top is the original.

Closer look at the spirit helpers in the top right of the picture helping the earthbound souls who wanted to cross over. There are many spirits here especially the little girl circled in the corner with pony tails. You can refer to the whole picture on page 28.

Below is the full original picture. I circled some of the spirits to show you where they were in the breakdown pictures. At the table are two boys talking, a girl with braids is underneath the table, a large dog is walking away from the table. In front of the statue and in the corner you will find a little girl with pigtails, a boy walking through the statue, and several others around. To the right of the picture going all the way up to the spirit helpers were several spirits on their way to cross over. It's an amazing picture!

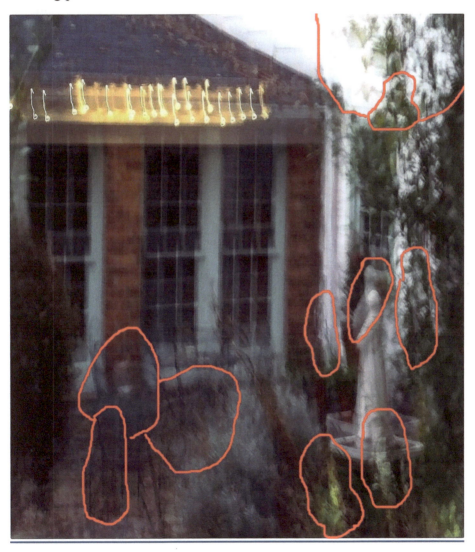

Legend and History of Fort Frederick

The stone fort, named in honor of Maryland's Lord Proprietor, Frederick Calvert, Sixth Lord Baltimore, was erected by Governor Horatio Sharpe in 1756 to protect English settlers from the French and their Indian allies. Fort Frederick was unique because of its large size and strong stone wall. Most other forts of the period were built of wood and earth. The fort served as an important supply base for English campaigns. During 1763, an Ottawa Indian chief named Pontiac forged a massive Indian uprising. Several hundred settlers and militia force sought protection within the fort during this brief uprising. Fort Frederick saw service again during the American Revolution as a prison for Hessian (German) and British soldiers. In 1791, the State of Maryland sold the fort. For the next 131 years, the fort and surrounding lands were farmed. During the Civil War, Union troops were often stationed around the fort to guard the C & O Canal. Taken from website: http://www.dnr.state.md.us/publiclands/western/fortfrederick.html

My family and I were looking for something to do in the winter months and often would get in the car and drive in a direction We ended up at Fort Frederick in Maryland and since it was winter the buildings were closed and we could just tour the inside of the fort for free. The buildings inside the fort were closed and really set up nicely from what I could see inside the window. As I was taking a picture through the window of one of the buildings, I later found that there were two spirit soldiers floating behind me. We were the only ones in the fort at that time, no one else was around.

" Floating Red Coats"

Spirit Photography taken at Fort Frederick, MD

Legend and History of The Landon House

Built in 1754, footsteps can be heard clearly when the house is vacant, doors close without provocation, and strange noises can be heard. Doors open and close by themselves often, lights turn on, music comes from the ball room. It was a plantation home in the civil war, which was used to treat soldiers hurt at the monocracy battlefield. There are slave quarters in the basement and a little church out back.

- The Landon House was built along the Rappahannock River in Virginia as a silk mill in 1754. It was relocated to Urbana, Maryland in 1840 where it became The Shirley Female Academy and then the Landon Military Academy & Institute.

- It was during the Confederates' first Maryland campaign that Landon would make history as the host site of legendary Confederate cavalry General J.E.B. Stuart's famous ball on September 8, 1862

- The Sabers and Roses Ball remains one of the high-water marks of the Confederacy since immediately following the ball all romantic notions of the Civil War ended at the Battle of Antietam, the bloodiest single day in American History.

- The house served as a hospital for both Union and Confederate troops and still has original signed and dated Civil War "lightning sketches" on the walls, drawn by Yankee and Rebel soldiers.

- History from the "Landon House website" www.landonhouse.com

The two boys that materialized look like they are ready for the ball at the mansion. One boy is in gray clothing with white collar and blonde hair. On the right standing next to him is another boy in a black dress coat sash and dark hair. In the trees and looking their way to the right, is a solider watching over them.

Original Photograph

Below as if posing for a picture in the middle, is a fluffy white dog with a red collar. Next to the dog and behind on the porch were two children who were starting too materialized in full form.

This picture was taken during Landon's House Friday Ghost Tours in 2006. We captured several spirits on the porch wanting recognition. Also, there was no one inside the house when this photo was taken according to Landon tour guides who were with me at the time this photo was taken. To the left in the window was a spirit shadow of a soldier inside the house. You will also find a Lady wearing a "ball gown" to the right at the stairway, there is a child coming out of the doorway, another solider materializing part way to the left of the picture and another solider sitting on the porch to the right. Yes, the person in the middle wearing a yellow jacket was a real person.

LEGEND OF MOUNT ST.MARY'S COLLEGE & GROTTO

Father John DuBois is sometimes seen walking the campus. Several Ghosts have been seen in dorms Brute and DuBois. This school has a history of ghosts and it is the oldest independent Catholic college in the country. It was founded in 1808. In the picture below to the left of the church materialized a spirit wearing red robes and who could be the spirit of Father John DuBois. In the next couple pages are other spirits we captured at Mount Saint Mary's.

Spirit Photography taken at Mount Saint Mary's. In the middle of the picture, is a man wearing a suit/dress coat who is pointing at me. I always wondered if he was trying to tell me "Hey, there's someone behind you!"

Going down the stairway path towards the college, there are two stone pillars where I captured a man dressed all in black with a mustache and long black hair looking directly at me. He is circled to the left of the pillar. In the middle of the pillars were several spirits just starting to materialize, peaking through the veil between worlds.

LEDGEND & HISTORY OF CATOCTIN FURNACE

- A good grade of hematite ore was discovered in the Catoctin Mountains in the 1770s by Thomas Johnson Jr., the first governor of Maryland. The Catoctin Furnace started producing iron in 1776. The fuel for the furnace was initially charcoal and the Catoctin forest provided the fuel for the furnace until 1873. Then the furnace was converted to coal. The remains of these iron works are found at the base of the Catoctin Mountains in Cunningham Falls State Park
- History from the website of: "The Catoctin Iron Furnace"
- In the following pages are the spirits we captured at the park and ruins.

Here in between the trees you can see just the face and beard of a soul. Directly across from him and a little up to the right, is a spirit leaning against the second tree that seems to be wearing a pointed hat. Both spirits are looking out amongst the woods.

Walking the path through the forest you are always being watched by spirits. Below is man taking a stroll and in the background are two children talking.

This was the first picture that I took and realized that I could capture spirits in my photographs, even those from mystical worlds. It was my first ever ghost tour that I attended. It was a night tour so I circled the spirits that materialized.

This is a frozen frame from actual footage from a video. Even though this picture is a bit blurry, it shows two angels, a woman in front wearing pink with a heart on her shirt, the other behind her coming into focus was another angel that was wearing armor, tall and strong who I feel was (Archangel Michael).

Again pictured below are more spirits hiding in the trees looking towards me for a photo. Walking through these woods is always relaxing. These spirits never mean any harm.

There are ruins of the main house not far from the furnace. I always seem to get a picture of spirits in this area. Pictured above the ruins of a pillar was a boy peeking out. When you look closely, you can see several other spirits too. Spirits tend to blend in with nature and their surroundings.

THE SPIRITS OF MONOCACY NATIONAL BATTLEFIELD

On the morning of July 9, 1864, Confederate and Union forces engaged each other along the banks of the Monocacy River. Although the battle was a military victory for the Confederates and their only victory in the north, it was also a defeat. The time spent fighting the battle cost the Confederates a crucial day of marching and provided the Union time to send reinforcements to Washington, D.C. General Early's army returned to Virginia and the remainder of the war was fought on southern soil. Because of General Wallace's valiant delaying action, the Battle of Monocacy became known as "The Battle that Saved Washington, D.C."

 Taken from website: For more history and tours of the battlefield go to: https://www.nps.gov/mono/learn/historyculture/battle_aftermath.htm

One thing I know for sure is that a lot of souls are still walking the trails and still fighting the war "Earthbound".

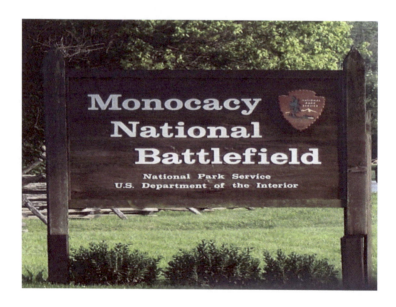

On the walkway as I was returning to the car I captured two spirits along the way. Below I captured a little girl walking towards me on the pathway and a solider just starting to materialize by the tree walking towards the girl.

This was the second picture I took as I was passing the little girl who was starting to disappear (shadow figure). Another solider to the left of the tree materialized on the ground with a bayonet through him and looking right at me.

This picture was taken in September where the spirit soldiers seemed like they were still fighting the war. Every time I get spirit souls in a photograph it still amazes me. Below are the soldiers looking our way and surprisingly one solider appeared riding a horse across the bridge.

This park is full of spirits. As I was leaving I captured these spirits on my cell phone camera. In the middle is a woman who is enjoying the sun. There is a young boy to her right who is dressed in a military outfit and looking at her. To the left of the women is a face of a little girl looking towards the spirit in the middle. Peaking around the tree to the right is a boy also dressed in a military outfit.

This recent photograph was at the same walking trail that has the most spirit activity. As I was exiting the trail, I felt as if someone was watching me, I then turned quickly and captured the spirit of a soldier who was just starting to come into focus. He has a beard and you can see his uniform and glint of a buckle on his pants.

This is the end of our adventure for now. Visit these sites referenced in this book and see what spirits you can encounter along the way. Below is a recapture of my favorite Ghost Visions photographs.

Spirits are as curious about us as we are about them. As seen below, they will follow you! Above my friend's head is a spirit that attached itself to her and two children on both sides. When dealing with spirits, get professional training on how to clear yourself and how to handle them if they do follow you home. Most will follow you to a certain point and then return back to their original site with their spiritual family. Some spirits are afraid of us and hide as you will see in some of the photos, they are afraid that we may try to pass them into the light. They never mean any harm to us in any way.

Thank you for supporting "Ghost Visions, LLC" and letting us share with you our stories and photographs.

We have more history and unique stories and experiences on our New Market Ghost Tours.

Please visit our website at www.ghostvisions.com for more information about us and upcoming Spirit Photography Classes, full moon and wine tours, investigations and upcoming books. Visit Ghost Visions on Facebook for the most recent pictures and updates on events.

Other Books Published by Ghost Visions.

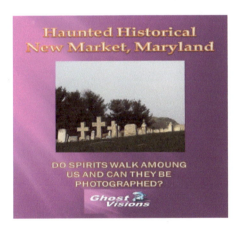

CPSIA information can be obtained
at www.ICGtesting.com
Printed in the USA
LVHW071556060421
683571LV00001B/2